ISO 10002
Certification

For all
Travel Agencies

Jahangir Asadi
Vancouver, BC CANADA

Published by: Silosa Consulting Group Inc.
Vancouver, BC **CANADA**
Email: Info@Silosa.ca
WWW.SILOSA.CA

Ordering Information:
Quantity sales. Special discounts are available on quantity purchases by universities, schools, corporations, associations, and others. For details, contact the "Sales Department" at the above mentioned email address.

ISO 10002 Certification for all Travel Agencies/J.Asadi —1st ed.
ISBN: 978-1-990451-96-6 Paperback

Contents

The system is working for you (the system is fully integrated along your processes and eases your operations).

You are working for the system (the system is beside your operations and looks as an additional burden.)

What is ISO 10002 ?

The International Organization for Standardization is an independent, non-governmental organization, the members of which are the standards organizations of the 165 member countries. It is the world's largest developer of voluntary international standards and it facilitates world trade by providing common standards among nations. More than twenty thousand standards have been set, covering everything from manufactured products and technology to food safety, agriculture, and healthcare.

What is ISO 10002 - CUSTOMER SATISFACTION?
Manage customer complaints effectively and you'll have more chance of meeting their expectations as well. And you can quickly turn customer complaints into customer satisfaction instead – especially when you view complaints as an opportunity to improve what you do and how you do it.

ISO 10002 can help you to achieve this whatever the size or nature of your business. The customer complaints management system is a basic but essential requirement for any business – especially businesses that want to become and remain successful.

Customers expect more and more from the service you provide. And your competitors are working harder to meet these expectations. You can too with ISO 10002, the international standard for customer satisfaction. It provides you with guidelines for putting in place your own complaints management system – helping you to identify complaints, their cause, and how to eliminate them.

ISO 10002 will also allow you to identify areas in your business where you can improve and eventually remove the cause of complaints. The standard outlines management controls and processes that help you to handle customer complaints more effectively and efficiently – making sure that more customers are satisfied with the service you provide.

More information can be obtained :

www.ISO.org

Who	Customers, Employees, Suppliers, Competitors, Govenrment
What	Strategy (Corporate, Business Unit, Marketing Product)
Where	Markets, Facilities, Distribution, Outsourcing
When	Strategic Plan. Annual Plan, Proogram and Projct Management
Why	Leadership, Communities, Culture, Change management
How	Marketing, Operating Pian, Sales Force, Metrtics, Incentives

17 Reasons why you need ISO 10002 Certification ?

1 Customer Confidence: By adopting the management system, ability to retain the loyalty of customers is enhanced. Customers feel confident of commitment for the resolution & redressal of any of their query or complaints.

2 Better Relationship: System helps to adopt a customer-focused approach to handle, analysis and review complaints and encourage personnel to improve their skills & behaviour in working with customers.

3 Continual improvement: Continual improvement of processes and re-sulting operational efficiencies mean money saved.

4 Brand Improvement: Certified complaint management system demonstrates to customers & other stakeholders that recognizing and addressing the needs and expectation of complainants, you have processes in place to handle, analyse and review complaints to improve the product and customer service quality.

5 Customer Satisfaction: Enhance customer satisfaction by creating a customer-focused environment that is open to feedback (including complaints), resolving any complaints, and enhancing the organization's ability to improve its product and customer service.

6 Improved Efficiency: Implementation and certification ensures a consistent process to handle customers, which enable to identify causes and eliminate the causes of complaints, as well as improve organization's operations.

7 Transparent System: Provide complainants with an open, effective and easy-to-use complaints process.

8 Auditable System: Complaint management system is auditable, thus auditing o f the complaints-handling process gives accuracy of the system compliance.

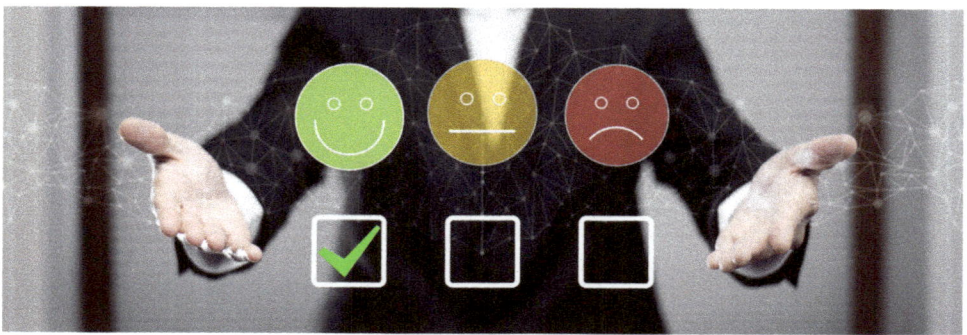

9 Synchronisation: It is developed as guidance for an organization's complaints handling process. It can be used alone or in conjunction with ISO 9001- Quality Management System of Organization.

10 Management System: This is a management system, therefore, all ingredients of management system are inherited in the complaint management system compliant to ISO 10002, reviewing the effectiveness and efficiency of the complaints-handling process.

11 Management Focus: Management commitment through adequate acquisition and deployment of resources, including personnel training;

12 Credibility: Effective complaint Management system helps to ensure defined responsibilities & procedures to handle & review complaints are in place.

13 Improve Company, Product and/or Services Quality: A quality management system standard is all about quality (really!) so, of course, one result of adopting a QMS should be an improved level of quality for the entire organization — every process, and every product.

14 Describe, Understand, and Communicate Your Company Processes: The standard requires that you identify and describe your processes using business metrics, the purpose of which is to better manage and control your business processes.

15 Develop a Professional Culture with Better Employee Morale: Implementing an Quality Management System can empower employees. Your QMS will provide them with clear expectations (quality objectives and job descriptions), the tools to do their job (procedures and work instructions), and prompt, actionable feedback on their performance (process metrics).

16

Improve Operational Consistency: What is consistent quality? Well, one way to think of it is "decreased variation". Reducing the variation in your processes is the definition of consistency. Is your customer better served by you supplying them with a consistent product — same dimensions, same weight, same tolerances, same output every time — or by your products being unpredictable and "all over the place"? (I hope you're not thinking too hard on this.) Of course, they won't accept variation, and neither should you! And how do you decrease variation? Increase control of your processes! Control comes from having a clear target to shoot for (objective), collecting data on the process (metrics), and understanding how to adjust the process (procedures and work instructions) to maintain the target output. If your QMS is working, you should be increasing operational… and product consistency.

17

Reduce Waste, and Save Money: A Quality Management System isn't perfect; no process and no one is perfect. Why else would the standard devote a clause to "continual improvement"? A well-run QMS does enable your company to approach perfection. As your processes improve, become more consistent, and you achieve your target objectives with greater regularity, you will see tangible results. Your process waste will decrease, for one. Waste is money lost forever. Waste results from poor quality and inefficiency. Inefficiency results from variation and inconsistent processes. Reduce variation, improve consistency, and you'll have less waste… and more money. It's that simple!

Who can be Certified to ISO 10002 ?

ISO 10002 Complaints Management System provides guidance on the process of complaint handling which includes planning, design, operation, and maintenance of complaint management within an organization. It can be used by any organization, large or small, regardless of its field of activity. In fact, there are over two million companies and organizations in over 170 countries certified to ISO Standards

All the requirements of ISO 10002 are generic and are intended to be applicable to any organization, regardless of its type or size, or the products and services it provides. ISO 10002 standard are applied to a wide variety of businesses globally. For all companies and organizations and different industries:

Accounting, Aerospace, Agriculture, Computers, Construction, Education, Economics, E-commerce, Engineering, Environmental Technology, Food, Forestry, Financial Services, Hospitality, Health care, Insurance, International trade, Investment, Law, Logistics, Media, Medical device, Natural resources, Pharmaceutics, Production, Robotics, Real Estate, Renewable energy, Research, Sales, Small business, Technology, Trade, ...

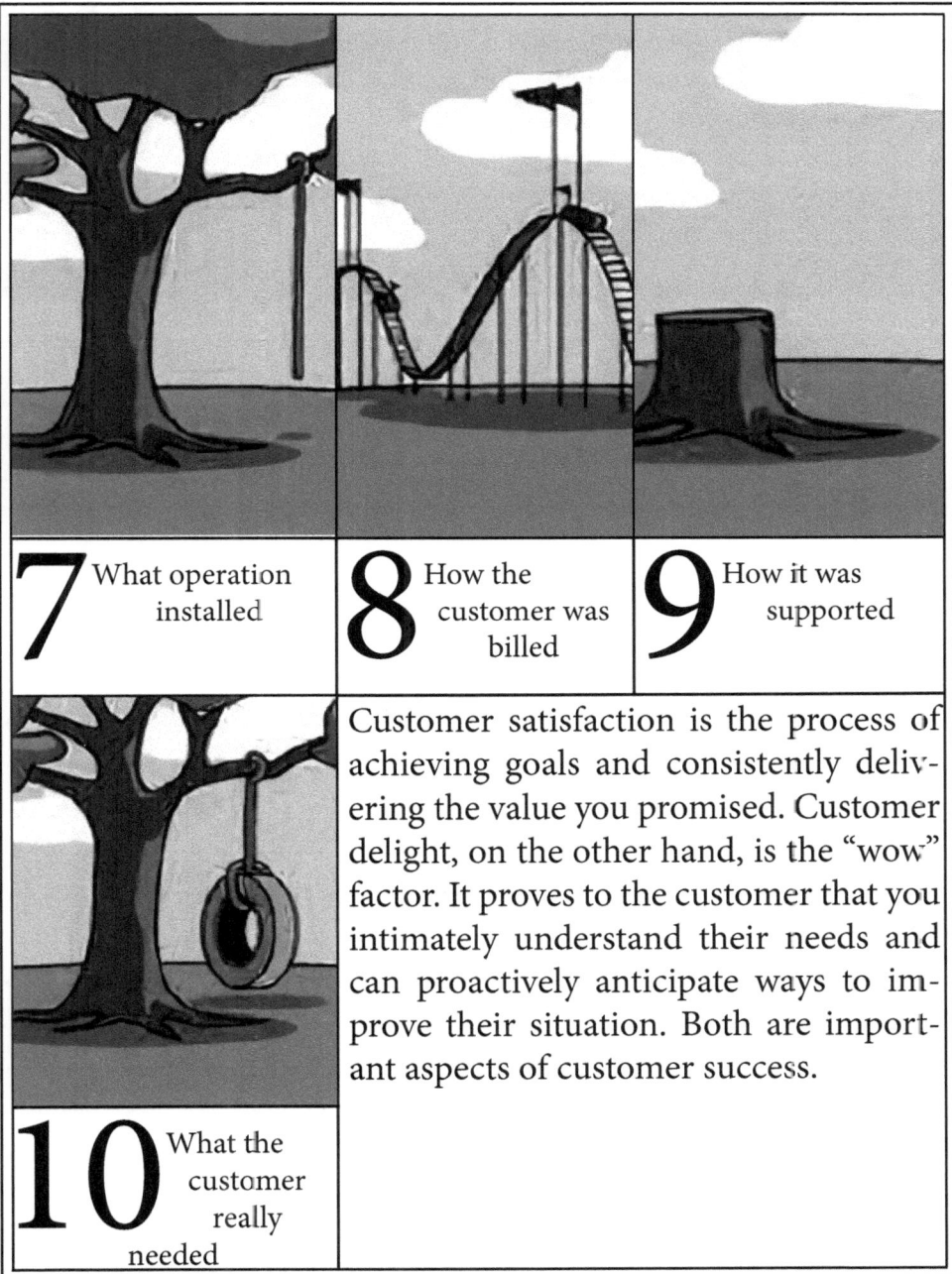

7 What operation installed

8 How the customer was billed

9 How it was supported

10 What the customer really needed

Customer satisfaction is the process of achieving goals and consistently delivering the value you promised. Customer delight, on the other hand, is the "wow" factor. It proves to the customer that you intimately understand their needs and can proactively anticipate ways to improve their situation. Both are important aspects of customer success.

What is an IAF Code? International Accreditation Forum, Provides Standard Industrial Classification: A code number representing certain types of industries and company types. IAF Codes are used to "hone in" the scope of your company›s business, so a Certification Body like GGC auditor with appropriate experience can be assigned to your company.

IAF	Description	USA SIC	Canada
1	Agriculture, fishing	01, 02, 07, 08, 09	1
2	Mining and Quarrying	10, 13, 14	2
3	Food products, beverages and tobacco	20, 21	3
4	Textiles and textile products	22, 23	4
5	Leather and Leather products	31	5
6	Wood and wood products	24	6
7	Pulp, Paper and paper products	26	7
8	Publishing companies	27	8
9	Printing companies	27	9
10	Manuf. of coke and refined petroleum products	29	10
11	Nuclear fuel	-	11
12	Chemicals, chemical products and fibers	28	12
13	Pharmaceuticals	28	13
14	Rubber and plastic products	30	14
15	Non-metallic mineral products	32	15
16	Concrete, cement, lime, plaster, etc.	32	16
17	Basic metals and fabricated metal products	33, 34	17
18	Machinery and equipment	35	18
19	Electrical and optical equipment	36	19
20	Shipbuilding	37	20

USA SIC 8 Digit Code - A 8-digit Standard Industrial Classification code identifying a line of operations for a business at the most specific level. Local Activity Type Code - A Dun & Bradstreet code identifying the type of activity code (i.e., 1987 SIC Code) represented in the Primary Local Activity Code field.

IAF	Description	USA SIC	Canada
21	Aerospace	37	21
22	Other transport equipment	37	22
23	Manufacturing not elsewhere classified	39	23
24	Recycling	95	24
25	Electricity Supply	49	25
26	Gas Supply	49	26
27	Water Supply	49	27
28	Construction	15, 16, 17	28
29	Wholesale and retail trade: Repair of motor vehicles, motorcycles and personal and household goods	50-59	29
30	Hotels and restaurants	54, 70	30
31	Transport, storage and communication	40-48	31
32	Financial intermediation; real estate; renting	60-67	32
33	Information Technology	35	33
34	Engineering services	87	34
35	Other Services	72-89 minus 87	35
36	Public administration	91-97	36
37	Education	82	37
38	Health and social work	94	38
39	Other social services		39
40	Medical Devices, medical products		40

Secret of Effective Management System Documentation

When you develop any documentation, verify it with the following rules:

5 W's & 1 H

If your document can answer these 6 questions, then you have developed a completely effective document; no matter that it is a quality manual, procedure, SOP, work instruction,.......

Who, When, Where, Why, What and How

Document required for ISO 10002

System Manual, System Procedure, Policy, Objectives, Mission & Vision, Standard Operating Procedure (SOP), Checklist, Forms Formats, Records

The extent of Documented Information differs as per:

- Organization's size
- Activities performed by the organization
- Processes undertaken by the Organization
- Products and services offered by the organization
- The complexity of processes undertaken
- Competence of persons involved

Role of **SCG** & Process of ISO 10002 Certification

SCG adopts a results-oriented approach to effective system implementation in the organization. A simple and practical method of system implementation helps organizations increase business efficiency and sustainability. SCG supports effective pre-audit to obtain a certificate of success in addition to enhanced performance.

The implementation process is described in the next page:

Time Frame	Task
Day 1	GAP Analysis Certification Body Selection Cost Estimates
Week 1	Developing Documents
Week 4	Implementing Management System
Week 8	Internal Audit MRM CAPA
Week 10	Certification Body Audit N-C Closing
Week 12	Certificate Issued
Year on Year	Yearly Compliance

Process
Finding the GAP between existing system related to ISO requirements Selecting the appropriate certification body Based on the scope of your business & certification body you choose
Management System Manual, Management System Procedures, Policy, Objectives, Forms etc. Review of Standard Operating Procedures (SOP)
ISO Awareness training for the top management and staff Implementing a well-documented management system throughout the organization
Internal audits identifying nonconformities related to ISO requirements Management Review Meetings Corrective and Preventive Action plan for nonconformities
CB acts on your behalf and assists you in the third-party audit Closing of any nonconformities identified by the certification body
ISO certificates issued for 3 years Surveillance Audits yearly
Support of Yearly documentation for audit

Bibliography:

Anttila, J., & Jussila, K. (2017). ISO 9001:2015- a questionable reform. What should the implementing organisations understand and do? Total Quality Management and Business Excellence, 28(9-10), 1090-1105. https://doi.org/10.1080/14783363.2017.1309119.

Astrini, N. (2018). ISO 9001 and performance: a method review. Total Quality Management & Business Excellence, doi: 10.1080/14783363.2018.1524293.

Bou-Llusar, J. C., Escrig-Tena, A. B., Roca-Puig, V., & Beltra´n-Martı´n, I. (2005). To what extent do enablers explain results in the EFQM excellence model? International Journal of Quality & Reliability Management, 22(44), 337-353.

Chatzoglou, P., Chatzoudes, D., & Kipraios, N. (2015). The impact of ISO 9000 certification on firms' financial performance. International Journal of Operations and Production Management, 35(1), 145-174. https://doi.org/10.1108/IJOPM-07-2012-0387

Chiarini, A. (2017). Risk-based thinking according to ISO 9001:2015 standard and the risk sources European manufacturing SMEs intend to manage. The TQM Journal, 29(2), 310-323. https://doi.org/10.1108/TQM-04-2016-0038.

Domingues, J. P. T., Sampaio, P., & Arezes, P. M. (2016). Integrated management systems assessment: a maturity model proposal. Journal of Cleaner Production, 124, 164-174, doi: 10.1016/j.jclepro.2016.02.103

Gigante, N., & Ziantoni, S. (2015). L'edizione 2015 della norma ISO 9001, 2015. Retrieved from:https://www.accredia.it/app/uploads/2015/12/6050_5_L__700_edizione_2015_della_norma_ISO_9001___Arch__Gigante__Dr__Ziantoni.pdf

ISO 10002 - Quality management systems – Customer satisfaction, Geneva: International Organization for Standardization.

ISO (2015). ISO Survey 2015 (online). Retrieved from: http//www.iso.org.

ISO (2018). ISO 19011 - Guidelines for auditing management systems quality management systems. Geneva: International Organization for Standardization.

ISO (2019). ISO 9000 Family - Quality Management. Retrieved from: https://www.iso.org/home.html.

Wilson, J. P., & Campbell, L. (2018). ISO 9001:2015: the evolution and convergence of quality management and knowledge management for competitive advantage. Total Quality Management and Business Excellence, pp. 1-16. https://doi.org/10.1080/ 14783363.2018.1445965

	# Easy ISO 9001:2015 Quality Management System
	# Easy ISO 13485:2016 QMS for Medical Devices
	# ISO 9001 for all Accounting Services ISO 9000 For all employees and employers
	# ISO 9001 for all Walk in Clinics ISO 9000 For all employees and employers

ISO 9001 for all
Local & International Schools

ISO 9000 For all
employees and employers

ISO 9001 for all veterinary Hospitals and Pet Clinics

ISO 9000 For all
employees and employers

ISO 9001 for all Day Care Centers and Kindergartens

ISO 9000 For all
employees and employers

ISO 9001 for all health and beauty Centers

ISO 9000 For all
employees and employers

ISO 9001 for all Pharmacies

ISO 9000 For all
employees and employers

ISO 9001 for all Plumbing Heating and AC Services

ISO 9000 For all
employees and employers

ISO 9001 for all Real Estate Industries

ISO 9000 For all
employees and employers

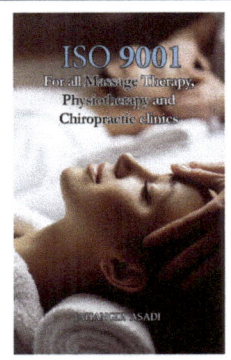

ISO 9001 for all Massage Therapy, Physiotherapy & Chiropractic Clinics

ISO 9000 For all
employees and employers

ISO 9001 for all Police Departments

ISO 9000 For all
employees and employers

ISO 9001 for all Banks and Financial Organizations

ISO 9000 For all
employees and employers

ISO 9001 for all Plumbing Heating and AC Services

ISO 9000 For all
employees and employers

ISO 9001 for all New and Used Car Dealerships

ISO 9000 For all
employees and employers

ISO 9001 for all Shopping Centers

ISO 9000 For all
employees and employers

ISO 9001 for all Fast food Restaurants

ISO 9000 For all
employees and employers

ISO 9001 for all Electrical Services and Industries

ISO 9000 For all
employees and employers

ISO 9001 for all Dental Clinics

ISO 9000 For all
employees and employers

ISO 9001 for all
Coffee and Pastry Shops

ISO 9000 For all
employees and employers

MDSAP Vol.1 to 5
Australia, Brazil, Canada, Japan, USA

ISO 13485 For all
employees and employers

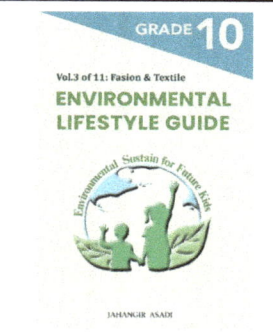

Environmental Lifestyle Guide
Vol.1 to 11

For all
Grade 9 to 12 Students

International Environmental
Labelling Vol.1 to 11

For all
employees and employers

International Manual of
Climate Change Control

For all People who wish to take care of Climate Change

CLIMATE CHANGE CONTROL
Special Price for Schools & Libraries

Exclusive Price via:
https://ecofriendlyeducation.com/

Online Education

Start your online course now after you have completed reading this book, do your quiz and receive your International Certificate via:

www.toptenaward.org

www.ingramcontent.com/pod-product-compliance
Lightning Source LLC
Chambersburg PA
CBHW051603120626
46551CB00013B/1646